THE STORY OF
MARS

BEN HUBBARD

W
FRANKLIN WATTS
LONDON • SYDNEY

First published in Great Britain in 2020 by The Watts Publishing Group

Copyright © The Watts Publishing Group, 2020

Editor: John Hort
Designer: Rocket Design (East Anglia) Ltd

HB ISBN: 978 1 4451 7281 1
PB ISBN: 978 1 4451 7282 8

Franklin Watts
An imprint of
Hachette Children's Group
Part of The Watts Publishing Group
Carmelite House
50 Victoria Embankment
London EC4Y 0DZ

An Hachette UK Company
www.hachette.co.uk
www.hachettechildrens.co.uk

Printed in Dubai

Picture acknowledgements:

Alamy/Mark Garlick 10.
NASA: 11bl, 53tr. NASA/GSFC: 8, 27t, 31b, 32-33t, 51tr, 61cl. NASA/GSFC/SVS: 20.
NASA/JPL: 16-17, 48-49, 51tl, 61cr. NASA/JPL-Caltech: 9, 34-35, 36-37t, 44b, 46c, 46-47t, 48br,
49cr, 52br, 52-53. NASA/JPL-Caltech/ESA/CXC/STScl: 17c. NASA/JPL-Caltech/MSSS: 4-5, 13,
29t inset, 42-43, 62-63. NASA/JPL-Caltech/University of Arizona: 21bl, 21br, 26-27, 30b,33br, 40-
41. NASA/Kim Shiflett.

Shutterstock: Alones 17br; John Andrus 40t; Baldas1950 58binsert; John A Davis 56-57;
Dotted Yeti, elements furnished by NASA 48-49cb, 60-61, 64b; Elena11, elements furnished by
NASA 1, 22-23; erancle 30-31bg; E71lena 54-55; Fabiobispo3D 50-51b; Irodphoto 37br; Sasa
Kadrijevic, elements furnished by NASA 24-25; Sebastian Kaulitzki 39; MN Studio 38b; Mopic
18-19t; Pike-28, elements furnished by NASA 35c; prait2512 58br; Vadim Sadovski, elements
furnished by NASA: 6-7, 14-15, 19br; Radoslav Stoilov 48-49ct, 64t; SunPhotography 23c;
3Dsculptor 44-45; WR Studios front cover; Yotam and sons 28-29t; Dima Zel,
elements furnished by NASA 2-3.

Every effort has been made to clear copyright. Should there be any inadvertent omission,
please apply to the publisher for rectification.

The website addresses (URLs) included in this book were valid at the time of going to press.
However, it is possible that contents or addresses may have changed since the publication of
this book. No responsibility for any such changes can be accepted by either the author or the
publisher.

All facts and statistics were correct at the time of press.

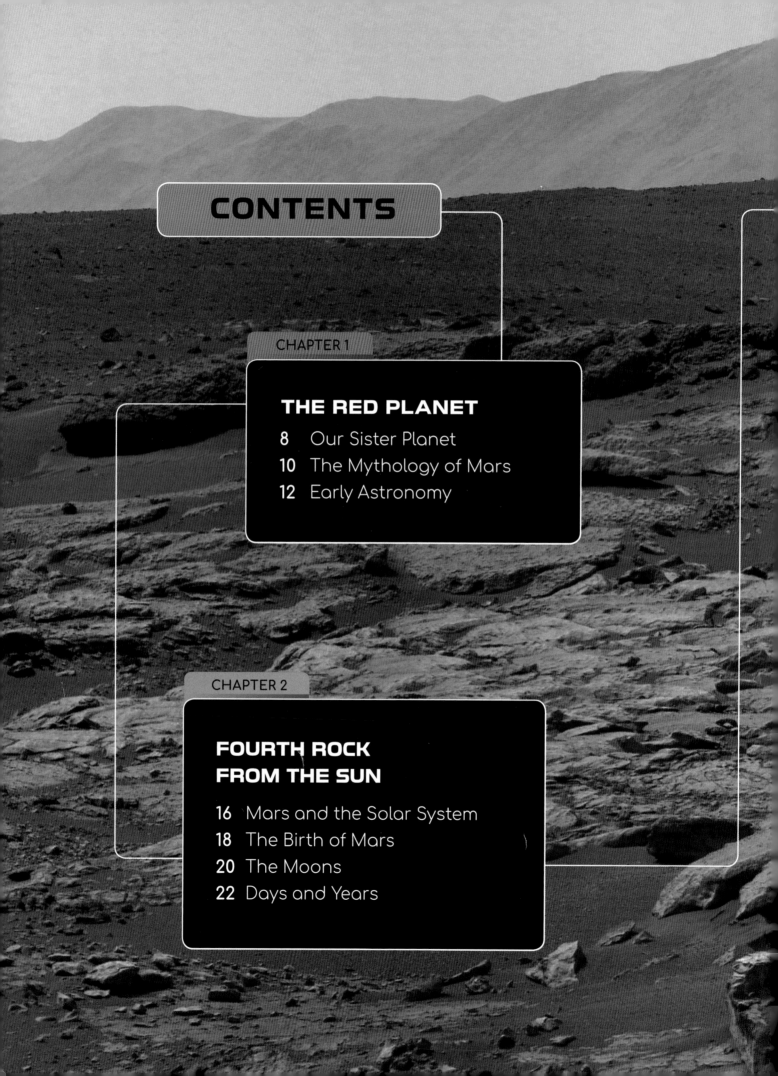

CONTENTS

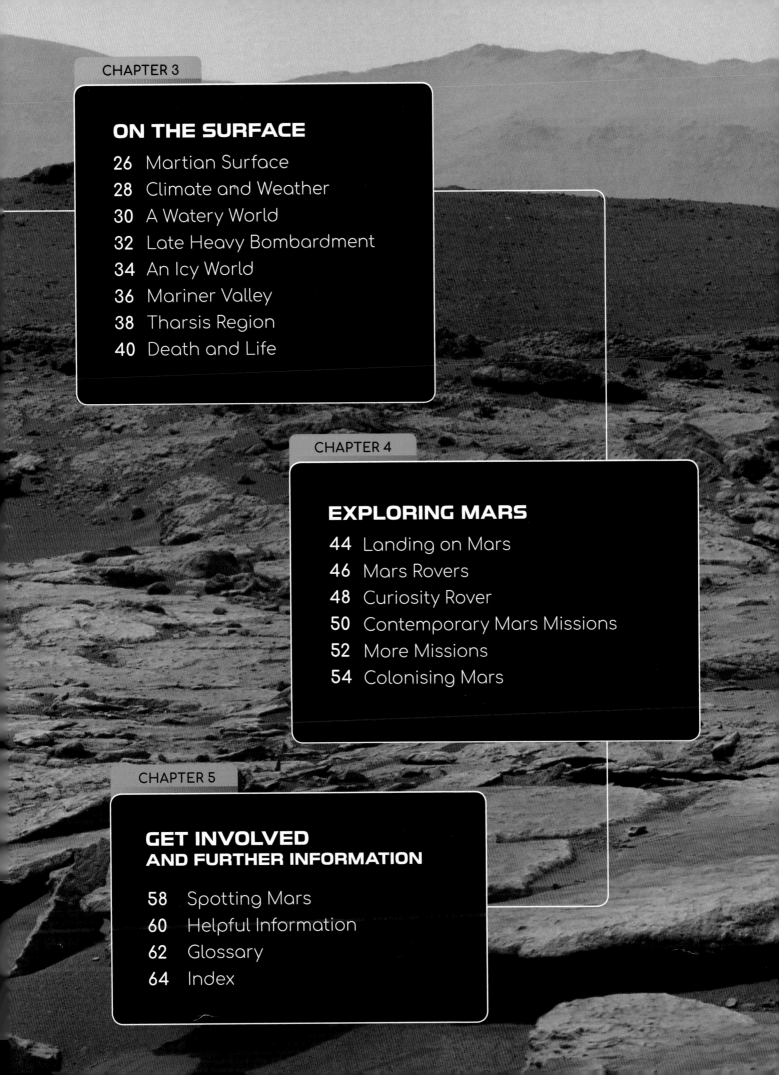

THE RED PLANET

OUR SISTER PLANET

On a cloudless night we can see a pale, red point shimmer in the black sky beyond us. This is not a star but a planet much like our own. It has a core made of rock and a surface covered with valleys, mountains, volcanoes and polar ice caps. It even has seasons, just like on Earth. Some say it is our sister planet. We call it Mars.

But unlike Earth, Mars is not a blue planet that has bustled with life for billions of years. Instead, it is a cold, barren world cloaked in a parched, red dust. There is no life on Mars that we know about, but perhaps beneath the arid surface there is some evidence of ancient, primitive creatures. Many scientists believe this is likely, because Mars was not always the dead, dry place it is today. Billions of years ago it was a world covered in lakes, rivers and oceans. Back then, the red planet was blue.

HG Wells vividly describes a Martian invasion in his 1898 novel, where the Martians use a robot called 'The Fighting Machine' to take over the planet.

THE MYTHOLOGY OF MARS

Thousands of years ago, people looked up at the red planet and imagined a place of blood, fire and destruction. The ancient Romans named the planet Mars, after their god of war. They believed Mars travelled wherever it wanted across the universe, like a wandering star.

Centuries later, authors wrote about the existence of alien beings on Mars. Many writers imagined Martians as advanced, hostile beings with a secret plan to invade the Earth. In 1898, HG Wells described a Martian attack on Earth in his famous novel, *The War of the Worlds*. His work later inspired many modern astronomers and rocket scientists, who wished to explore space.

In 1976, the Viking 1 space probe took a photo that appeared to show a face on the surface of Mars. Some believed this was a massive sculpture built by Martians, like the pyramids on Earth. However, the face turned out to be an illusion, created by shadow and light on a hill in the planet's Cydonia region.

EARLY ASTRONOMY

Science fiction writers were not the only ones who believed there was intelligent life on Mars. Many scientists agreed. In 1877, Italian astronomer Giovanni Schiaparelli observed a series of dark, criss-crossing lines on Mars through his telescope, which he called 'canali'. This was wrongly translated into 'canal' rather than 'channel' in English, so many people assumed the lines were waterways, purposely dug to transport water.

In the early twentieth century, American astronomer Percival Lowell built on this theory. Lowell wrote books insisting that Martians were desperately building canals to transport the last water on their dying planet from the polar ice caps to their cities. Lowell convinced many people with his theories, but other astronomers were doubtful. Later, as the century developed, new technologies enabled astronomers and scientists to make great breakthroughs in their understanding of Mars.

EARLY MARS OBSERVATION TIMELINE

2000 BCE
Ancient Egyptians first observe Mars, calling it 'Her Desher', 'the red one'.

CE 1610
Italian astronomer Galileo Galilei makes the first telescopic observation of Mars.

CE 1666
Giovanni Cassini records white spots at Mars' poles, which he assumes are made of ice.

CE 1783
William Herschel correctly theorises that Mars' tilt gives it seasons, like on Earth.

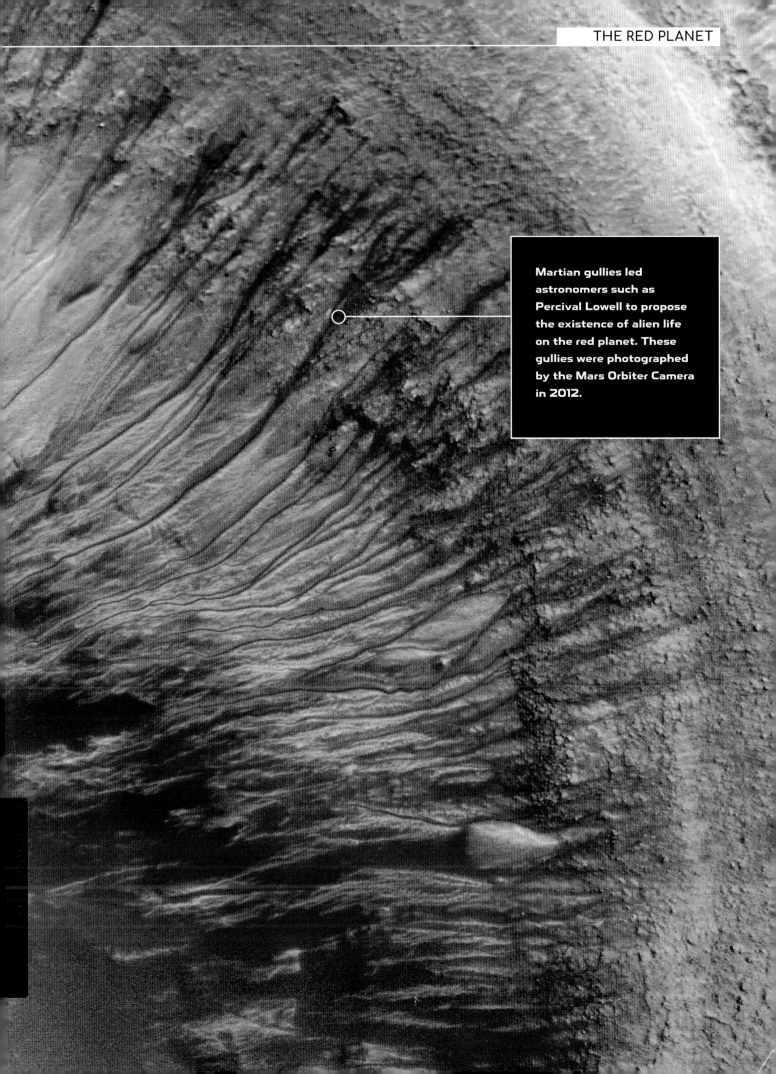

Martian gullies led astronomers such as Percival Lowell to propose the existence of alien life on the red planet. These gullies were photographed by the Mars Orbiter Camera in 2012.

FOURTH ROCK FROM THE SUN

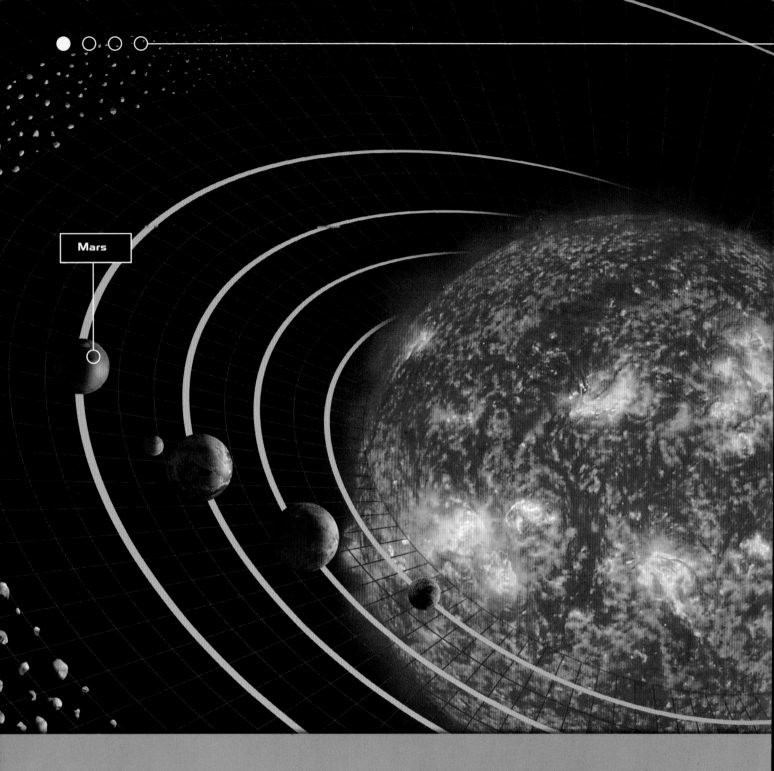

Mars

MARS AND THE SOLAR SYSTEM

Mars is one of eight planets in orbit around our nearest star, the Sun. This group of planets and the Sun is called the solar system. Mars is the fourth planet from the Sun and is one of the four rocky planets.

Mars' nearest neighbours are Mercury, Venus and Earth. Hundreds of millions of kilometres further away lie the four outer planets: Jupiter, Saturn, Uranus and Neptune. Beyond these 'gas giants' stretches the vast expanse of space.

The Milky Way

MARS

Our Sun is only one of over 100 billion stars grouped together into a galaxy called the Milky Way. The Milky Way and 54 other galaxies make up a cluster of galaxies known as the Local Group. There are thought to be more than 100 billion other galaxies in the universe, which is continuing to expand.

DATA FILE

- Size: 7th largest planet in solar system
- Diameter: 6,791 km
- Distance from the Sun: 229 million km
- Average orbiting speed around the Sun: 23 km/sec

An artist's impression of the early solar system.

THE BIRTH OF MARS

Mars was born around 4.6 billion years ago during the formation of the solar system. At that time, the solar system was a swirling disc of gas and rock, which spun rapidly around the newly-ignited Sun. Over millions of years, enormous chunks of rock collided with each other – some crashed apart and others clumped and gravitated together. Some of the larger chunks collected increasing amounts of rock, until they formed the small embryos of planets. One of these embryos gained more mass and grew into Mars.

Mars' core is mainly made of a mixture of iron and sulphur.

Mars has an internal structure like Earth's. It is made from three distinct layers: a metal core surrounded by a rock mantle and covered with a thin, rocky crust.

Billions of years ago, Mars' metallic core and its rotation caused a magnetic field around the planet, much like the one found on Earth. This protected it against harmful particles fired out from the Sun. However, around 4 billion years ago, Mars' magnetic field stopped working. From that point on, Mars began to lose its atmosphere and became the barren world we know today.

Phobos

THE MOONS

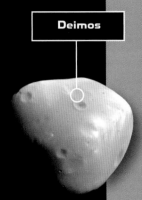

Deimos

Mars has two moons in orbit around it: Phobos, meaning 'fear'; and Deimos, meaning 'terror'. Unlike the Earth's round Moon, Phobos and Deimos are much smaller, irregular-shaped lumps of rock.

Phobos, the larger of the two, has a rugged surface covered with impact craters where objects, such as meteorites, have struck it. The largest of these craters is nearly as wide as the moon itself.

Deimos, by comparison, is a smaller, smooth world with few craters. It moves in a more distant orbit around Mars than Phobos, meaning it may one day fall out of its orbit completely and drift away into space. Phobos, on the other hand, may get closer and closer to Mars, causing it to one day collide with the planet. The resulting debris may cause Mars to develop planetary rings, much like Saturn's. However, this will probably not happen for another 50 million years.

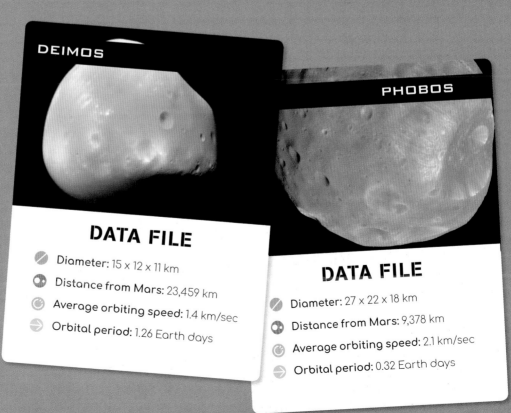

DEIMOS

DATA FILE

- Diameter: 15 x 12 x 11 km
- Distance from Mars: 23,459 km
- Average orbiting speed: 1.4 km/sec
- Orbital period: 1.26 Earth days

PHOBOS

DATA FILE

- Diameter: 27 x 22 x 18 km
- Distance from Mars: 9,378 km
- Average orbiting speed: 2.1 km/sec
- Orbital period: 0.32 Earth days

21

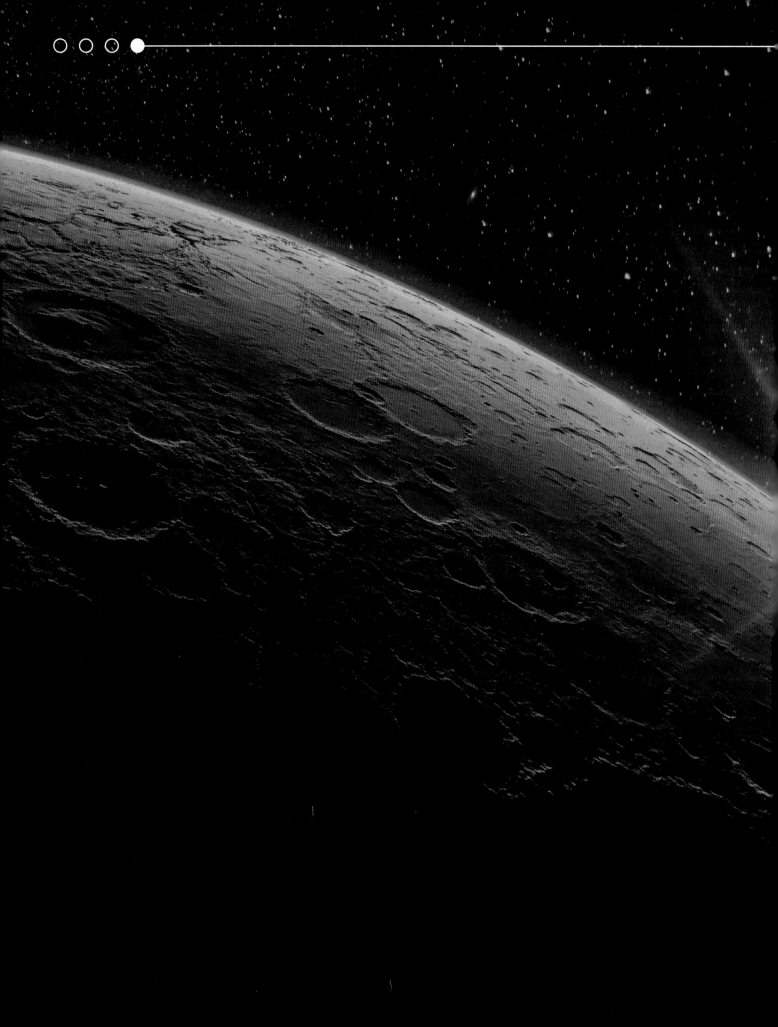

DAYS AND YEARS

The time it takes for a planet to make one full rotation on its axis is known as a day. During this time, half the planet is illuminated by the Sun and the other half is stuck in the shade. We know these times as day and night. Mars makes a full rotation every 24 hours and 39 minutes, making its day slightly longer than on Earth.

Mars is around 50 per cent further away from the Sun than Earth. This means it takes Mars longer to complete a single orbit, which, in turn, makes its year longer than on Earth. A Mars year lasts for 687 days, instead of the 365 we experience on Earth.

DAY LENGTH ON OTHER PLANETS

DATA FILE

Day length on other planets

Mercury:
1,408 hours

Venus:
5,832 hours

Earth:
24 hours

Mars:
25 hours

Jupiter:
10 hours

Saturn:
11 hours

Uranus:
17 hours

Neptune
16 hours

ON THE SURFACE

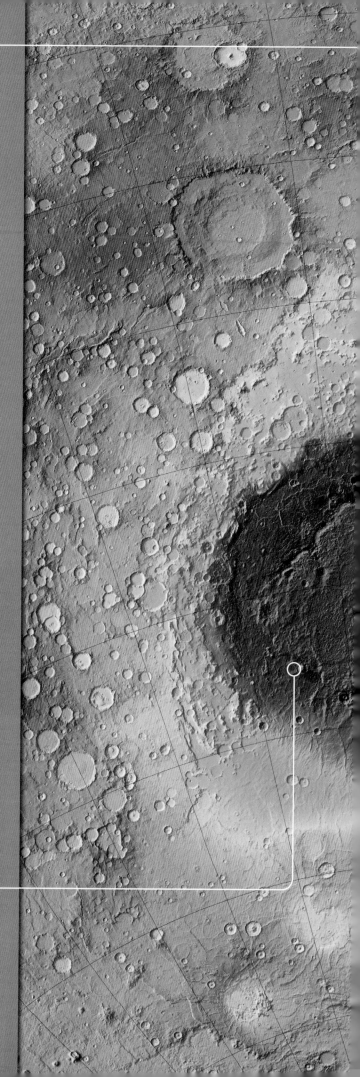

MARTIAN SURFACE

Compared to Earth, Mars is a dead planet. Its waters have disappeared and its volcanoes lie extinct. Rocks and a rusty-red dust cover the planet; the thin atmosphere means there are no clouds, so rain cannot wash the dust away.

Unlike Earth, Mars has stopped evolving. The history of the planet is therefore etched into its surface. Its flat plains are pockmarked by massive impact craters, caused by asteroids from outer space. Valleys, riverbeds and basins have been left carved into the rock by the water which once filled them. These geographical landmarks remain unchanged from the time they were formed, sometimes billions of years ago.

This topographic map of Mars uses colours to show the contours of the surface. The purple circle is the deep crater of Hellas Basin (see p33).

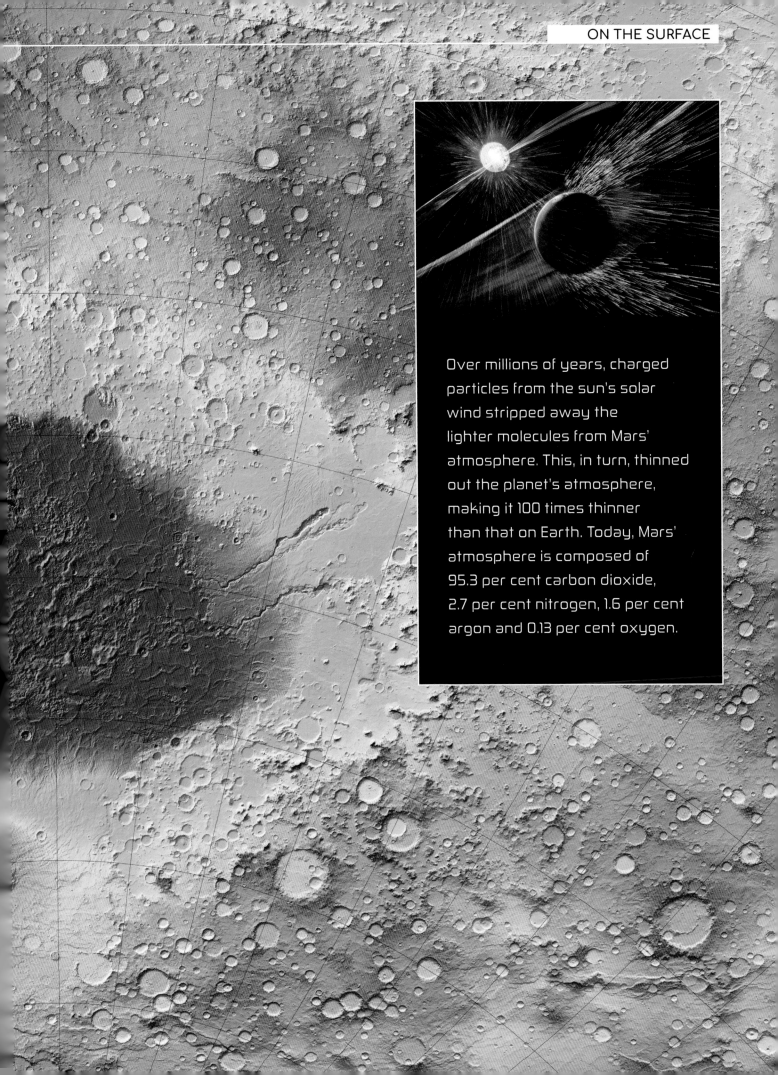

Over millions of years, charged particles from the sun's solar wind stripped away the lighter molecules from Mars' atmosphere. This, in turn, thinned out the planet's atmosphere, making it 100 times thinner than that on Earth. Today, Mars' atmosphere is composed of 95.3 per cent carbon dioxide, 2.7 per cent nitrogen, 1.6 per cent argon and 0.13 per cent oxygen.

CLIMATE AND WEATHER

Despite only having a thin atmosphere, Mars still has a climate. Because it is tilted on its axis, like the Earth, Mars experiences seasons. The half of the planet leaning towards the Sun has a summer, while the other half has a winter. The seasons then change as Mars travels along its orbit. However, Mars is further from the Sun than the Earth and has only a thin atmosphere to contain heat. Temperatures on the surface therefore range from −140°C to a maximum of 30°C.

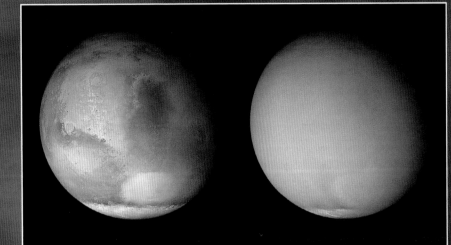

These two images of Mars were taken from the same position a month apart. The right image shows the planet almost completely covered in a dust storm, hiding all the detail of the surface. Dust storms can reach more than 60 km high during planet-wide storms.

The weather on Mars is dry and windy, especially during the six months of summer when large, dust storms rage for months on end. Fuelled by a mix of warm equatorial air and cold polar air, Mars' dust storms can reach wind-speeds of 100 km/ph and cover the entire planet. A large Martian dust storm can even block out the Sun.

Wind is not the only weather on Mars. Although there is no rain, it does sometimes snow. Martian snowflakes, however, are not made from water, but carbon dioxide. The snowflakes are also smaller than those found on Earth, leading in many cases to a type of 'fog effect', rather than looking like falling snow.

ERIDANIA BASIN

The Eridania basin was home to Mars' largest lake. Covering an area of 1.1 million square km with a depth of 1.5 km, it was almost three times larger than Earth's largest lake, the Caspian Sea. Eridania Lake is thought to have contained warm, hydrothermal vents (see p40) and a mixture of minerals, including iron, magnesium and calcium. Scientists were very excited by this finding. On Earth, life first began in mineral-rich areas around hydrothermal vents under seas and oceans. Could life, therefore, have also been produced in the Eridania basin?

An image of the Eridania basin today.

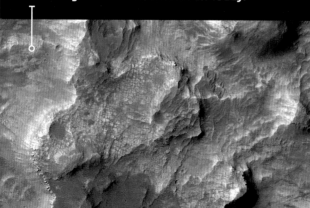

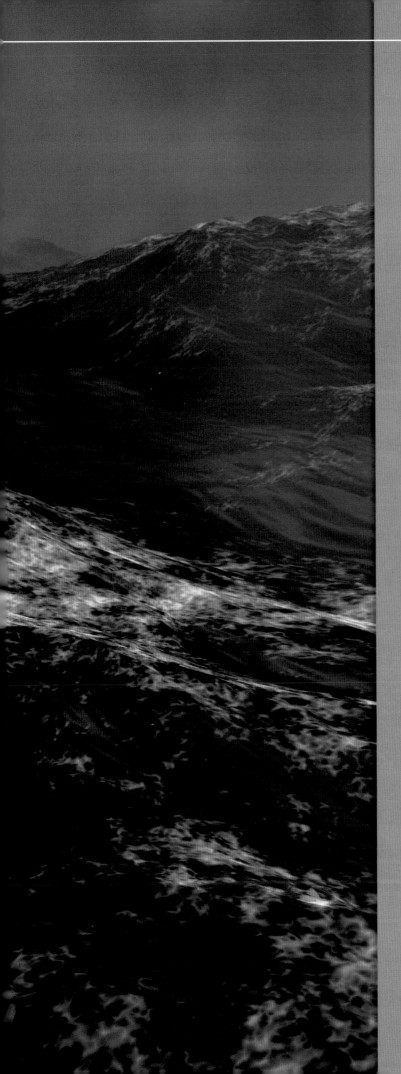

A WATERY WORLD

Mars was not always a dry, dead world. Four billion years ago, it was a wet, warm planet with a thick atmosphere. During this era, known as the Noachian Period, streams trickled down from the planet's highlands and standing water collected in large, interconnected lakes. Vast rivers 2 km wide and 2,000 km long carved their imprints into rocky valleys, and seas washed over 25 per cent of the planet's northern hemisphere.

This is how Mars may have looked four billion years ago – surprisingly similar to Earth!

LATE HEAVY BOMBARDMENT

Around 4.1 billion years ago, a period of spectacular violence struck the solar system. Massive asteroids left over from the planet-building period slammed into larger worlds, leaving their surfaces scarred. Known as the Late Heavy Bombardment, this assault on the planets lasted for tens of millions of years and brought Mars to the brink of destruction.

During the bombardment, countless asteroids broke up into burning chunks of rock which crashed into the Martian surface. It is estimated that over 53 tonnes of rock fell on every square metre of Mars during this time,

BOMBARDMENT CAUSE

No one can be sure what caused the Late Heavy Bombardment. Some scientists think it may have occurred when Neptune moved outwards towards the Kuiper Belt – a massive ring of rocky, icy objects at the edge of the solar system. Neptune's gravity may then have disrupted these objects, sending them inwards towards the planets.

obliterating over 30 per cent of its surface. Impact craters, such as the Hellas basin, remain to tell the tale. Hellas is the largest visible impact crater in the solar system: it is over 22,000 km in diameter and 9 km deep. You could drop Mount Everest into the Hellas basin and look down on its highest peak.

An image from NASA's Mars Reconnaissance Orbiter shows the rim of a huge 50-km-diameter crater near the Hellas basin.

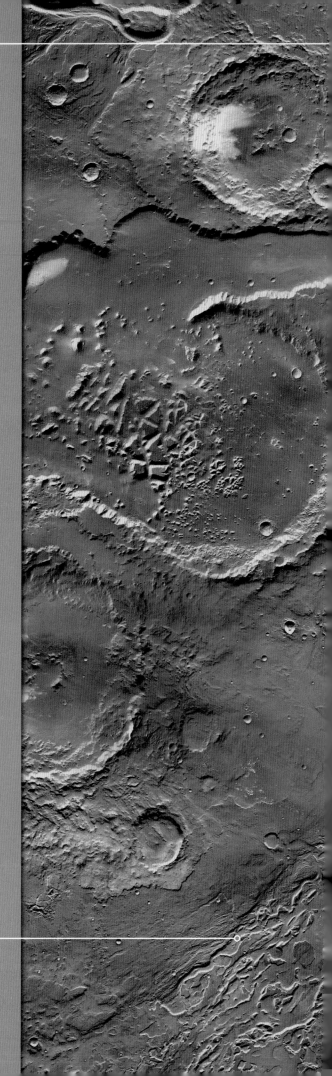

AN ICY WORLD

Around 3.5 billion years ago, Mars began to change from a warm, wet planet to the cold, arid world we know today. As Mars' atmosphere thinned, its temperatures plunged. The planet entered a deep freeze, known as the Hesperian Period. During this time, rivers ran dry and much of the planet's standing water was locked into ice. However, increased volcanic activity melted the ice in some regions, which unleashed the solar system's most spectacular floods.

One such flood started in the planet's volcanic highland, known as the Tharsis region. An eruption at Tharsis melted a reservoir of ice, unleashing over 350,000 cubic metres of water into the Echus Chasma valley below. This created a waterfall over 4 km high. That's four times higher than the highest waterfall on Earth, Brazil's Angel Falls.

The surface of Mars has been scarred by torrents of water caused by melting ice.

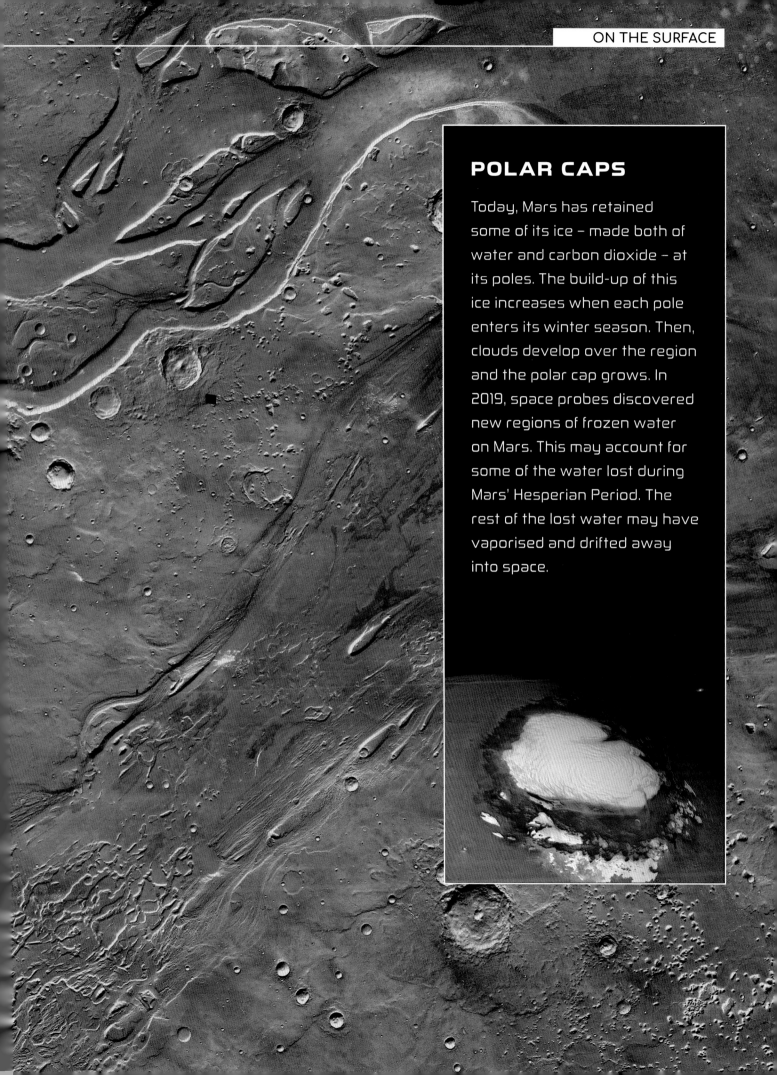

POLAR CAPS

Today, Mars has retained some of its ice – made both of water and carbon dioxide – at its poles. The build-up of this ice increases when each pole enters its winter season. Then, clouds develop over the region and the polar cap grows. In 2019, space probes discovered new regions of frozen water on Mars. This may account for some of the water lost during Mars' Hesperian Period. The rest of the lost water may have vaporised and drifted away into space.

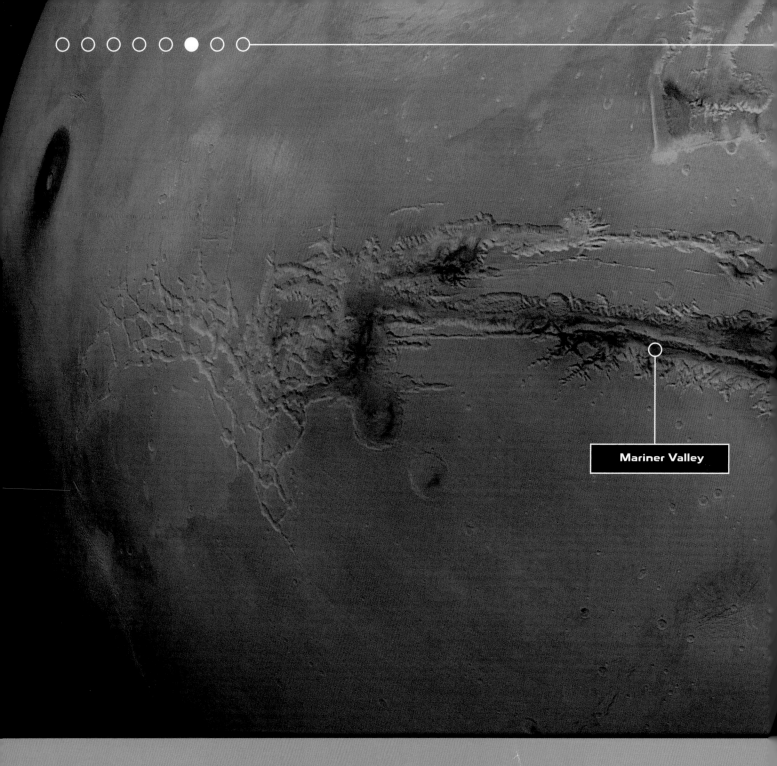

Mariner Valley

MARINER VALLEY

Mariner Valley is a deep, wide gash that cuts a swath across the surface of Mars. It is one of the largest canyons in the solar system. Lying just below the planet's equator, the valley is over 4,000 km long, 200 km wide and more than 10 km deep.

Mariner Valley was probably created around 3.5 billion years ago by the same volcanic and tectonic movement that formed the volcanoes of the Tharsis region. As molten rock pushed up to form these volcanoes, Mars' crust cracked, creating the early Mariner Valley.

EARTH'S GRAND CANYON

The Mariner Valley dwarfs the largest canyons on Earth, including America's Grand Canyon. However, the Grand Canyon is still impressive at 446 km long, 30 km wide and 1.6 km deep.

Over time, floodwaters created heavy erosion and landslides that enlarged the valley. The floodwater then carved a network of side channels as it rushed down into low-lying areas. This created the valley as we see it today.

THARSIS REGION

As its Hesperian Period drew on, Mars became a quiet, frozen world with little surface activity. That is, except for its volcanoes, which began a period of explosive eruptions. At this time, the great volcanoes of the Tharsis region blasted rock and ash high into the air and sent searing hot clouds of poisonous gas and lava rushing down their mountainsides.

Lying at the edge of the Tharsis region is the largest volcano in the solar system: Olympus Mons. Over 22 km high and 624 km across, Olympus Mons has a crater, or caldera, that is 85km wide. Olympus Mons obtained its enormous size partly from eruptions of fluid, basaltic lava. This lava ran down the shield volcano's sides and built it up over millions of years.

MAUNA LOA

The shield volcanoes of the Tharsis region would tower over the tallest volcano on Earth, Hawaii's Mauna Loa. Tiny in comparison to a Mars volcano, Mauna Loa stands 4 km above sea level and is around 120 km across.

Olympus Mons

LIFE ON EARTH

No-one knows if there was life on Mars, but the discovery that the planet once had hydrothermal vents in its seas and oceans is an encouraging sign. On Earth, these same vents created life in a perfect chemical soup of water, heat, minerals and gas. However, if there was some form of life on Mars it was probably not as complex as the animals we see on Earth today. Instead, Martian life may have been some sort of single-celled microbe. Perhaps this life lies still hidden deep beneath the planet's surface.

Wind is a powerful force on Mars. It blows loose sand across the surface, carving features into the landscape. These features are known as yardangs.

DEATH AND LIFE

After millions of years of violent activity, the volcanoes of Mars went out. Around 2.9 million years ago, Mars ended its Hesperian Period and entered its Amazonian Period. During this time, water vaporised at the planet's surface and its seas and oceans disappeared, as much of Mars' water was lost into space. Winds blew sediment, sand and soil across its vast, flat plains. A dust containing high levels of rusty iron blanketed the planet and turned it red. If life had ever existed on Mars, it was now gone.

Around two billion years ago, when Mars was largely a dead planet, there was already complex multi-cellular life on Earth. Ironically, Earth had begun its existence as an arid, lifeless planet with a toxic atmosphere; now it had reversed its fortunes with Mars.

EXPLORING MARS

LANDING ON MARS

For decades, un-crewed missions have been sent to Mars to try and unlock its many secrets. Landers, orbiters and rovers have studied the planet looking for clues about its mysterious past. They hope to answer our most pressing questions: what happened to Mars' water, why did its atmosphere thin and did it ever contain life? The first crewed mission to Mars will aim to answer an even bigger question: could people ever live on the red planet?

In 1975, the Viking 1 and 2 probes were launched to explore Mars. The spacecraft would not only orbit the planet and beam back photos to Earth, but also drop landers onto its surface. The landers provided the first panoramic photos of Mars, revealing its rusty, red landscape under a salmon-coloured sky. The landers also collected soil in a scoop and tested it for organic matter. The tests, however, were inconclusive.

The Viking Project was the first US mission to land a spacecraft successfully on the surface of Mars.

MARS ROVERS

Mars rovers are robotic buggies that are built to traverse the planet's rocky terrain, take measurements and study samples of the soil and rock. The first rover, called Sojourner, was parachuted down to the planet in 1997 from the Pathfinder spacecraft. Powered by solar panels on its roof, the small rover survived for 83 days until communication with Earth was lost.

In 2004, Opportunity became the first of a new generation of Mars Exploration Rovers to touchdown on Mars. Equipped with a unique suspension drive system and a large array of solar panels, Opportunity was a serious advancement on Sojourner. The rover surpassed expectations: it survived dust storms by going into hibernation and kept itself operational by constantly recharging its solar batteries. Only expected to last for 90 days, Opportunity's mission continued for over 14 years before it succumbed to a dust storm. The rover discovered many smooth pebbles during its travels, which proved the previous existence of running water on the planet; the once-rough rocks would have been smoothed by rivers and oceans.

THE OPPORTUNITY ROVER

DATA FILE

- Length: 2.3 m
- Height: 1.5 m
- Weight: 185 kg
- Top speed: 0.14 km/ph
- Total distance travelled: 45.16 km

The surface of Mars taken from the front Hazard Avoidance Camera on NASA's Mars Exploration Rover, Opportunity.

OUT-OF-THIS-WORLD RECORDS!

Driving distances on Mars

0.1 KM Sojourner 1997

7.7 KM Spirit 2004–2010

20.4 KM Curiosity 2012–present

45.16 KM Opportunity 2004–2018

CURIOSITY ROVER

Launched in 2011, Curiosity is NASA's most ambitious rover to date. Just landing the USD$2.5 billion, 899 kg rover gently enough not to damage its precious instruments was a great feat of engineering. Because no one knew if it would work, the landing sequence was called 'seven minutes of hell'.

1 The rover was dropped into Mars' atmosphere inside a 'cruise stage' spacecraft. It reached speeds of 8,500 km per second and temperatures of 2,100°C.

2 At 11 km above the surface, the cruise stage slowed itself to 1,700 km/ph by deploying a parachute. Its heat shield fell away.

3 The shell around the descent stage fell away. The descent stage fired its retro rockets.

4 At 19 m above the surface, long ropes called a sky crane lowered the rover from the descent stage.

5 The descent stage fired away so it would not land on the rover as it touched down. Landing was complete.

THE CURIOSITY ROVER

DATA FILE
- Length: 5.1 m
- Height: 2.2 m
- Weight: 899 kg
- Top speed: 0.14 km/ph

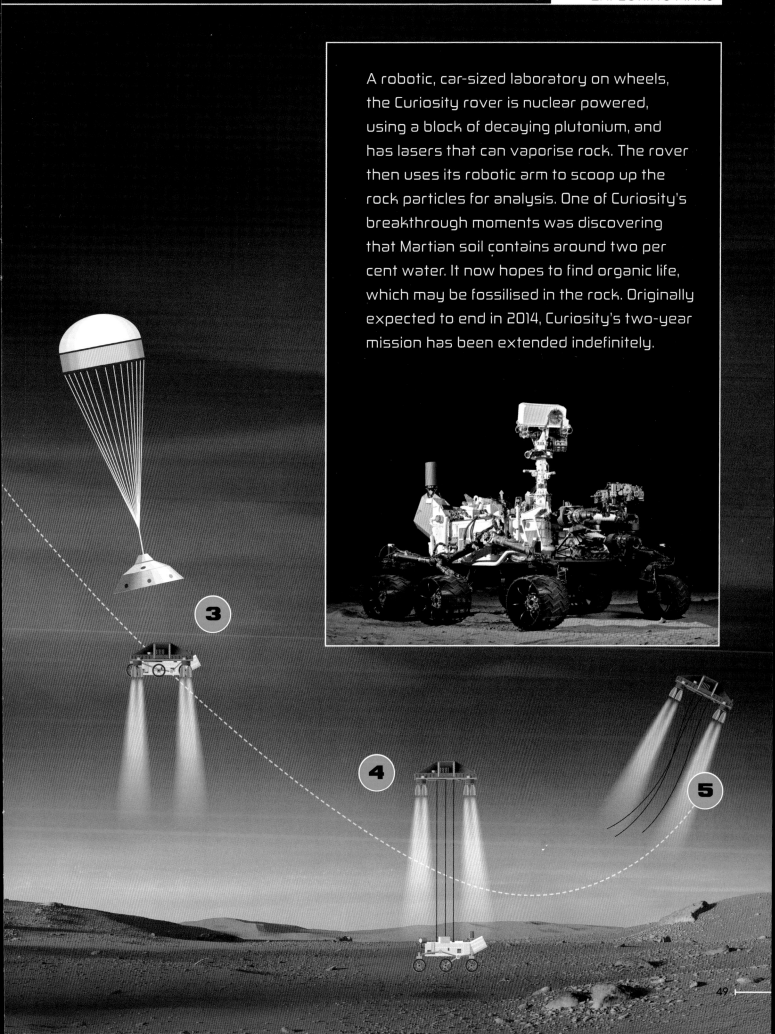

A robotic, car-sized laboratory on wheels, the Curiosity rover is nuclear powered, using a block of decaying plutonium, and has lasers that can vaporise rock. The rover then uses its robotic arm to scoop up the rock particles for analysis. One of Curiosity's breakthrough moments was discovering that Martian soil contains around two per cent water. It now hopes to find organic life, which may be fossilised in the rock. Originally expected to end in 2014, Curiosity's two-year mission has been extended indefinitely.

3

4

5

CONTEMPORARY MARS MISSIONS

Today, a fleet of Martian orbiters continue our study of Mars. As they circle the red planet, the orbiters beam back their findings to Earth. Many of these communications are sent via the Mars Reconnaissance Orbiter (MRO). Designed to map Mars' landscape in detail, MRO can photograph a feature the size of a football on the Martian surface with its high-resolution cameras.

EXOMARS

Unlike most other existing Mars missions, which have been launched by the National Aeronautics and Space Administration (NASA), the ExoMars programme is a European Space Agency (ESA) initiative. In 2016, ExoMars' Trace Gas Orbiter and Schiaparelli lander reached the red planet and began their studies of gases in its atmosphere. Two years later, a NASA lander called InSight joined Schiaparelli on Mars and began measuring the planet's seismic activity.

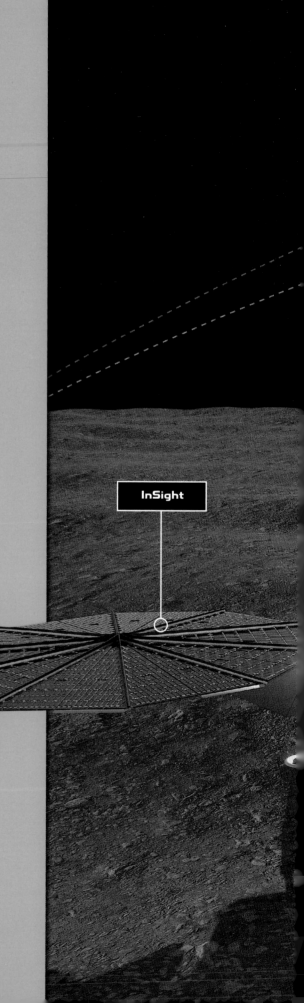

InSight

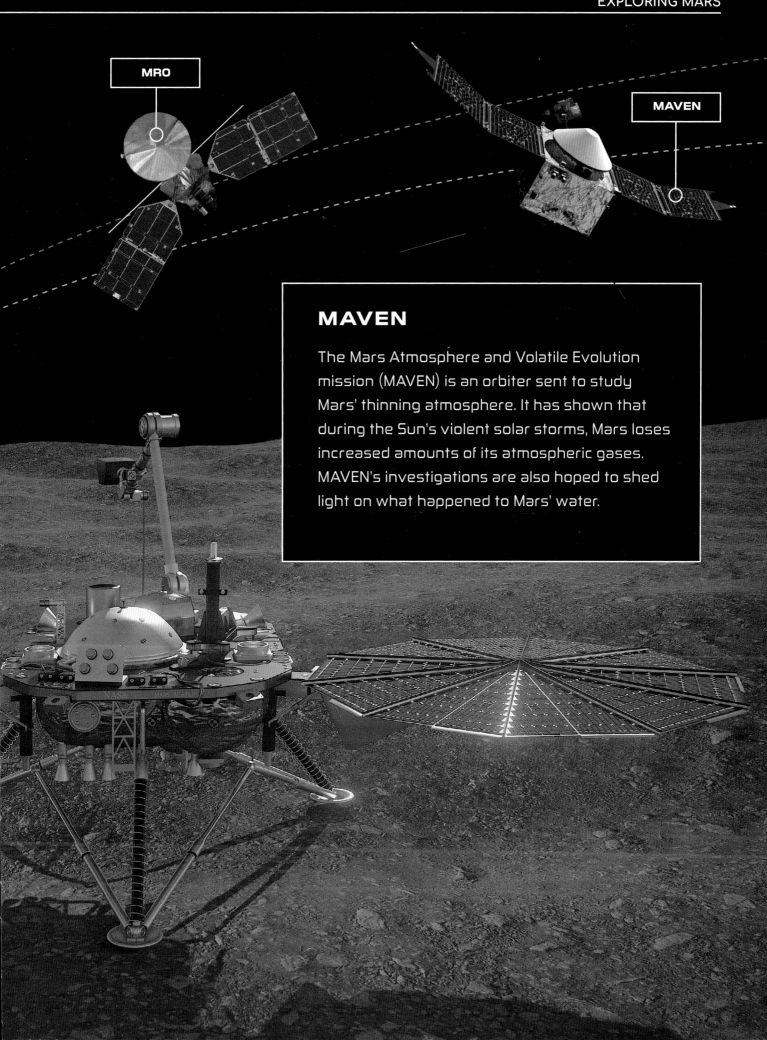

MRO

MAVEN

MAVEN

The Mars Atmosphere and Volatile Evolution mission (MAVEN) is an orbiter sent to study Mars' thinning atmosphere. It has shown that during the Sun's violent solar storms, Mars loses increased amounts of its atmospheric gases. MAVEN's investigations are also hoped to shed light on what happened to Mars' water.

MORE MISSIONS

Over the last few decades, our exploration of Mars has intensified. Missions to Mars are becoming more frequent and involving more countries than ever before. Russia, China, Japan, India, the European Union, the United Arab Emirates and the United States all have missions planned for the next few years. These include future plans for the first ever crewed mission to Mars.

An engineer working on the Mars 2020 rover.

MARS 2020 ROVER

NASA's Mars 2020 mission is a rover containing a small, drone-sized helicopter. Attached to the belly of the rover, the helicopter has solar-power and a twin-rotor to fly itself to hard-to-reach places such as caves, cliffs and deep craters. The helicopter is the first aircraft taken to another planet.

CREWED MISSION

NASA plans to send astronauts to Mars in the future by first sending them to a 'Gateway' space station in orbit around the Moon (right). However, the lunar Gateway launch is not planned until the mid 2020s. This is also the time that a private company called SpaceX has announced it wants to send its own crewed mission to Mars. The astronauts would fly aboard a spacecraft called Starship and then establish a base on Mars.

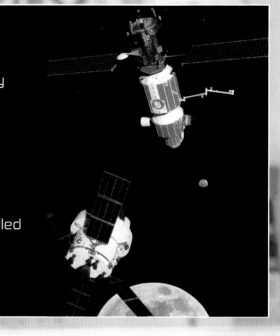

COLONISING MARS

Because Mars is so similar to Earth, it is thought that humans could one day live there permanently. However, Mars is currently not a hospitable environment for people. Temperatures drop to −140°C, dust storms rage across the surface for months at a time and there is no oxygen to breathe.

Life on Mars would be tough. A Mars base would most likely begin as a series of self-contained structures called modules, possibly built underground. The first modules would consist of a laboratory, a science module, a habitat module and a module to grow vegetables, such as lettuce,

beans and potatoes. Scientists think these vegetables would grow in the Martian soil. As more colonists arrived on the planet, more modules would be added, perhaps constructed using Martian dust and 3D printers.

Mining Mars for precious mineral resources would be vital in supporting human life on the red planet. Water ice could be melted for drinking and broken down into its chemical parts – hydrogen and oxygen – to provide air to breathe. Carbon extracted from the atmosphere could be used to make plastic, rocket propellant and fuel for heating. Life on Mars would be difficult, but not impossible.

GET INVOLVED
AND FURTHER INFORMATION

SPOTTING MARS

Mars is easy to see on a clear, cloudless night using only your naked eye. However, if you have access to binoculars or a telescope, then that is even better. Visiting a planetarium or observatory is the best way of all to get a close-up view of Mars.

HOW TO SPOT IT

Mars looks like a reddish-pink dot in the night sky. Exactly where it appears in the sky depends on the hemisphere and country you are looking from. The simplest way to pinpoint the planet is by downloading an app of the night sky (see p60). These enable you to pick out celestial objects by holding up a mobile phone to different regions of the sky. You can also use the old-school method – a map of the stars, which you can purchase in a book, or print out from the Internet.

WHEN TO SPOT IT

There are periods when Mars is closer to the Earth than others, as it travels around the Sun. At its closest point to Earth, Mars reaches a distance of 57.6 million km away. The last time that happened was in 2003 and it won't happen again for another 60,000 years. However, every 15–17 years it gets close enough for 'exceptional viewing' and a close approach happens every 26 months. See p60 for some websites that will give you tips on astronomy and stargazing.

HELPFUL INFORMATION

It's easier than ever these days to become a budding astronomer with child-friendly websites, apps and books. Check some out below:

STARGAZING AND ASTRONOMY WEBSITES

This NASA kids' website has fascinating facts and statistics about Mars:
starchild.gsfc.nasa.gov/docs/StarChild/solar_system_level1/mars.html

NASA's Kids Club website is all about the solar system and the planets:
www.nasa.gov/kidsclub/index.html

This ALMA telescope website is packed full of information for young astronomers:
kids.alma.cl

The Hubble space telescope website gives live and archived views of the cosmos as well as constellation guides:
hubblesite.org

This children's section of the Astronomy.com website has great information about the planets and stars:
www.astronomy.com/observing/astro-for-kids

This Smithsonian website has links to space travel for all age groups:
airandspace.si.edu/educator-resources

APPS

These free mobile phone apps allow you to point your phone at the night sky and identify star constellations and planets. A great way to find Mars!

SKY SAFARI
This award-winning app lets you identify celestial objects simply by holding your phone up:
skysafariastronomy.com

SKY VIEW
An augmented-reality app that uses your phone's camera to show planets, stars and constellations in the night sky:
www.educationalappstore.com/app/skyview-free-explore-the-universe

STAR WALK
Another educational astronomical tool that lets users explore celestial objects in real time through their mobile phone screen:
starwalk.space/en

SOLAR SYSTEM EXPLORER
This app is like a vast, hand-held planetarium that helps identify celestial objects:
www.educationalappstore.com/app/solar-system-explorer-lite

STARLIGHT
This app shows the most prominent constellations, stars and planets in the night sky and labels them:
play.google.com/store/apps/details?id=com.gyrocade.starlight&hl=en_GB

STAR CHART
Star chart provides a different way of observing the night sky by filtering by object, such as planets, stars or constellations:
apps.apple.com/gb/app/star-chart/id345542655

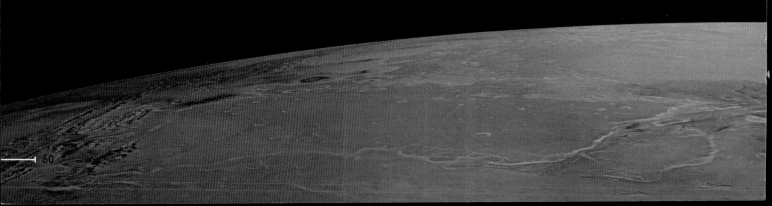

ASTRONOMY CLUBS

Joining an astronomy club can give you key insights into upcoming occurrences in the night sky, as well as tips on the best places to see them.

This Sky and Telescope website lets you find the closest astronomy club to you, wherever you are in the world:
www.skyandtelescope.com/astronomy-clubs-organizations

This NASA website is all about astronomy for children with links to astronomy clubs around the world:
spaceplace.nasa.gov/astronomy-clubs/en

BOOKS

Space: Planets Near Earth
Ian Graham, Franklin Watts (2016)

Space Science (series)
Mark Thompson, Wayland (2019)

Visual Explorers: Space
Paul Calver, Franklin Watts (2016)

Wonders of the Night Sky
Raman Prinja, Wayland (2021)

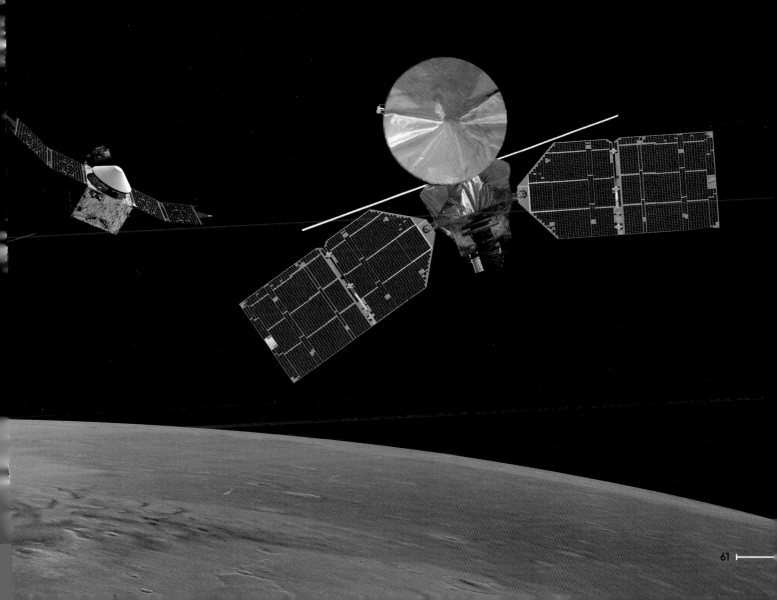

GLOSSARY

Asteroid A small rock that orbits the Sun.

Astronomy The study of space, celestial objects and the Universe.

Atmosphere The protective layer of gases that surrounds the Earth.

Basalt A type of volcanic rock.

Basin A circular valley on a planet's surface, often containing water.

Canal An artificially made waterway.

Carbon Dioxide A colourless, odourless gas that is poisonous to humans.

Celestial Object Something that is found in space, such as a planet or star.

Colonise To take over a place and settle there.

Core The central, innermost layer of a planet.

Cosmos Space and everything it contains.

Crater A large hole on the surface of a planet, moon or asteroid, usually caused by the impact of a meteorite.

Crust The outermost layer of a planet.

Cydonia A region on the planet Mars.

Diameter A straight line passing from side to side through the centre of a circle or sphere.

Embryo A thing at an early stage of its existence, with the potential of development.

Equator A line drawn around a planet that is an equal distance from both poles.

Etch Corrode, carve or eat into.

Evaporate Turn from liquid into vapour.

Fossil The remains or outline of a prehistoric planet or animal.

Galaxy A large group of stars, planets and other celestial objects found throughout the Universe.

Gas Giant A large planet that is made up mainly of gas.

Gullies Channels formed by the movement of water.

Hemisphere The north or south half of a world, which is divided by a central invisible line called the equator.

Hydrothermal Vents Gaps in the seafloor from which water from the crust of a planet, that's been heated by magma, mixes with seawater.

Lander A robotic craft which lands on another world but stays in one place.

Mantle The part of a planet's interior between the crust and the core.

Mass The amount of matter in an object.

Meteor A small icy or rocky object that usually burns up while entering a planet's atmosphere.

Meteorite A meteor that hits Earth's surface.

Milky Way The galaxy that contains our solar system.

Multi-cellular (life) Living things that consist of more than one cell, including all animals and plants.

Observatory A building equipped with instruments such as telescopes for use in astronomy.

Orbit A circular path around another object.

Orbital Period The time it takes for one object to complete one full orbit around another object.

Orbiter A robotic spacecraft designed to stay in orbit around another world.

Particle A tiny piece of matter.

Planetarium A domed building which images of celestial objects are beamed onto for public education and entertainment.

Plutonium A chemical used to fuel nuclear reactors.

Probe A robotic spacecraft that explores outer space.

Rover A robot that has been designed to explore the surface of another planet.

Science Fiction A story that is usually about futuristic things, such as science and technology.

Season The four parts of the year (spring, summer, autumn and winter), caused by a planet's changing position around the Sun.

Seismic Relating to earthquakes and other tremors.

Shield Volcano A type of volcano that is usually made up of lava flows.

Solar Panels A device made to absorb the Sun's rays and turn it into electricity.

Solar System The collection of eight planets and their moons, asteroids, and comets in orbit around the Sun.

Telescope An optical instrument which makes faraway objects appear closer.

Topographic Relating to the shape and physical features of land, such as valleys and mountains.

Vaporised To convert something into a gas.

INDEX